BEATITUDES – FRONT

LORD'S PRAYER – CENTER

OF THE SERMON ON THE MOUNT

Beatitudes – Front Lord's Prayer – Center Of the Sermon on the Mount

Copyright © 2023 Richard G. Manning M.D.. All rights reserved.

No rights claimed for public domain material, all rights reserved. No parts of this publication may be reproduced, stored in any retrieval system, or transmitted in any form or by any means, electronic, mechanical, recording, or otherwise, without the prior written permission of the author. Violations may be subject to civil or criminal penalties.

ISBN: 978-1-63308-724-8 (paperback)
       978-1-63308-727-9 (ebook)

Cover and Interior Design by *R'tor John D. Maghuyop*

1028 S Bishop Avenue, Dept. 178
Rolla, MO 65401

Printed in United States of America

BEATITUDES – FRONT
LORD'S PRAYER – CENTER
OF THE SERMON ON THE MOUNT

Contemplating Jesus' Call
to Suffer Joyfully for Righteousness

A Primer

Richard G. Manning M.D.

Table of Contents

Dedication 7
Front 8
Center 9
A Call to Contemplate God's Truths Together. 11
Introduction. 13
First Beatitude 20
First Part of the Prayer 21
Second Beatitude 22
Second Part of the Prayer 23
Third Beatitude 24
Third Part of the Prayer 25
Fourth Beatitude 26
Fourth Part of the Prayer 27
Fifth Beatitude 28
Fifth Part of the Prayer 29
Sixth Beatitude. 30
Sixth Part of the Prayer. 31
Seventh Beatitude. 32
Seventh Part of the Prayer. 33
The Order of the Mass 34
Eighth Beatitude. 36
Embolism. 37
Ninth Beatitude 38
Doxology 39
The End of the Sermon on the Mount 40
Sermon on the Mount Cross-verse Puzzle. 47
References 48

Dedication

To my wife

my co-laborer and prayer warrior

Front

Blessed are the poor in spirit, for theirs is the kingdom of heaven.

Blessed are they who mourn, for they will be comforted.

Blessed are the meek, for they will inherit the earth.

Blessed are they who hunger and thirst for righteousness, for they will be satisfied.

Blessed are the merciful, for they will be shown mercy.

Blessed are the clean of heart, for they will see God.

Blessed are the peacemakers, for they will be called children of God.

Blessed are they who suffer for the sake of righteousness, for theirs is the kingdom of heaven.

Blessed are you when they insult you and persecute you and utter every kind of evil against you [falsely] because of me. Rejoice and be glad, for your reward will be great in heaven. Thus they persecuted the prophets who were before you.

Center

Our Father who art in heaven,

Hallowed be thy name.

Thy kingdom come, thy will be done on earth, as it is in heaven

Give us this day our daily bread

And forgive us our trespasses, as we forgive those who trespass against us.

And lead us not into temptation,

But deliver us from evil.

Deliver us, Lord, we pray, from every evil, graciously grant peace in our days, that, by the help of your mercy, we may be always free from sin and safe from all distress, as we await the blessed hope and the coming of our Savior, Jesus Christ.

For thine is the kingdom, and the power, and the glory, now and forever, Amen!!!

A Call to Contemplate God's Truths Together

As I write this book, the world, especially Western Civilization, confronts a steadily advancing human secularism seemingly on the verge of destroying the ancient and time-honored Judeo-Christian beliefs, traditions, and practices on which we built this civilization. Stopping this Satanic-led onslaught will require a strong, sustained, loving, and unified Christian response- strong because Satan has an army of worldly-wise followers with immense resources at its disposal- sustained because Satan will not stop trying to thwart God's plan until the day of final judgment, the day He will be cast down into hell forever- loving because God is love- unified because that's how God planned to build His kingdom. Jesus seemed especially concerned with the last two, love and unity. Near the end of His three-year ministry, He said, *"This is how all will know that you are my disciples, if you have love for one another." (John 13:35)* His message is clear, requiring no explanation. Then, as the time for His arrest approached shortly after the Last Supper, Jesus expressed His strong desire for unity among His followers. *"I pray not only for them, but also for those who will believe in me through their word, so that they may all be one, as you, Father, are in me and I in you, that they also may be in us, that the world may believe that you sent me." (John 17:20-21)*

Surely, the Christian world must confront human secularism to reverse the world's chaotic declension, but the Church itself has become chaotic and disjointed and thus severely hampered to address this urgent need. Most assuredly, the failure to remain unified- all one in Jesus and the Father- lies not with God but with us, His scattered followers, His broken body, and His suffering Church. If this short meditation accomplishes nothing more than bringing Christians together around the words of their savior, it will have accomplished its' author's chief ambition.

May His Sermon keep us imagining and contemplating how to pray, speak and act to glorify Him. May we bless God together so God can bless us together with His people, the myriads of saints who ran their race ahead of us to build the foundation of love on which we stand. Amen!

Introduction

There are two thousand two hundred and thirty-nine words in the Sermon on the Mount. The first nine sentences, known as Beatitudes, contain one hundred-twenty words. The middle word, the one thousand one hundred and nineteenth of the Sermon on the Mount, is *'to,'* and the next is *'your.'* We find them in the sentence, *"But when you pray, go to your inner room, close the door, and pray to your Father in secret."* Of course, the counts I have presented here will vary depending on the biblical translation one uses. Still, these small differences do not detract from the point I want to focus on. The Beatitudes are at the front, and the Lord's Prayer, the Our Father, is in the center of the Sermon on the Mount. Perhaps, I have misused the idiom, which refers to one, not two positions. "Step forward, soldier, front and center." However, it should catch our attention, should it not, that we find in Jesus' first and longest recorded sermon the foundational words for finding the kingdom of heaven and the most famous prayer for asking God's help to find the kingdom of heaven in these conspicuous positions with a mere forty-eight verses separating them. If we were with the crowd on the mountain that day, five minutes, give or take a minute, would have transpired between when Jesus finished the Beatitudes and started the Prayer. Considering these observations, is it not evident that Jesus intends for those seeking the kingdom of heaven by walking the difficult way of the Beatitudes to seek God's help by praying the Our Father? And, is it not also evident that Jesus intends for those seeking to understand the meaning of the Beatitudes and the Lord's Prayer to start by contemplating them within the remaining words of the Sermon on the Mount?

Commentaries from the ancient up to our modern day explore the complementary relationship between the Beatitudes and the Lord's Prayer. Not surprisingly, one finds differences in the teaching of the relationship's nature, the number of Beatitudes Jesus spoke, and the number of parts in the Prayer. Further still, for the past five hundred years, many Protestants have included *"For thine is the kingdom and the power and the glory, now and forever,"* immediately after *"deliver us from evil,"* while Catholics pray the doxology after the priest at Mass recites the embolism, *"Deliver us, Lord, we pray, from every evil, graciously grant peace in our days, that, by the help of your mercy, we may be always free from sin and safe from all distress, as we await the blessed hope and the coming of our Savior, Jesus Christ."*

You have already seen how I arranged the front and center of the sermon. Instead of explaining why or how I came up with this order, I am simply providing space for you to contemplate the nine paired parts together. In providing this space for contemplation, I pray that Christians of many denominations will gather around a sermon that all agree on concerning its central importance to the Church of Jesus Christ. Surely, achieving a unified vision won't be easy. We must offer a sustained look at this Sermon on the Mount- an effort that explores the whole Bible and centuries of Church traditions, and in so doing, perhaps we can find the motivation to spend more time together and more and so on until we finally become what Jesus prayed for us to become. Only then will we be able to offer a strong antidote to the wiles of human secularism. Only then can we overcome the world with love.

I offer a few housekeeping items before getting started. First, to help in this contemplative effort, I have repeatedly asked the same eight questions, four concerning the Beatitude and four concerning the Prayer. I have set the pages up so that the reader holding an open book in their hands will see on the left page the Beatitude with its odd-numbered questions and on the right page, the part of the Prayer with its even-numbered questions. I have done this to encourage you to move back and forth from contemplating the Beatitude to the Prayer. Think of it as a conversation between Jesus and His Church. Certainly, one can and should think and pray through both the Beatitudes and the Prayer in their own sequence. Still, this book aims to replace that scriptural study paradigm with a contemplative effort that starts, continues, and finishes by considering the two twin towers of truth as a single unified unit of teaching.

To keep our initial contemplation focused on and guided by the Sermon in which Jesus spoke the Beatitudes and the Lord's Prayer, I have prepared the first five questions under the nine Beatitude/Prayer pairs using references from the Sermon on the Mount. I have used every phrase/word from the Sermon on the Mount just once and positioned them with the Sermon's front and central words in a way that I hope you find helpful in unpacking their dense truths. For the sixth question, under each of the nine pairs, I have referenced nine mountaintop experiences in Matthew's gospel which take us from the beginning to the end of his gospel. We leave Matthew's gospel for the seventh question under each pair to contemplate nine biblical characters and their families, starting with Adam and Eve, Abel, Noah, Abraham, Jacob/Israel and his twelve sons, Moses/Israel, David/Israel, John the Baptist/the Church, and Jesus and Mary. We aren't contemplating the characters and their families randomly, but rather, within the context of Matthew's gospel, especially as they relate to the Beatitude, the Lord's Prayer, and the verses from the Sermon on the Mount I have associated with them.

Because my non-Catholic Christian readers may not be familiar with the embolism or the doxology, I have provided a simple chart of the parts of the Mass to show where they fit into the Lord's Prayer and the liturgy. In addition, because a significant part of Catholic worship, especially at every Mass, involves the celebration of the sacraments, we will consider them in this contemplative effort. Instituted by Christ and manifest by Him in the Church's worship, the sacraments are the revelation of Jesus Christ, par excellence for Catholics. I provided references from the Catechism of the Catholic Church (CCC) for those wanting clarification on the Church's teaching about the sacraments. I believe it is the most reliable Catholic source concerning them. Mind you; these CCC references are themselves replete with scripture.

After contemplating the nine pairs, we bring this work to an end by contemplating the end of the Sermon on the Mount, which will complete the work you hold in your hands, but, hopefully, begin a sustained lifelong work of encountering Jesus' words as most Christians have to date. Few would have read His words in the first fifteen centuries after Christ's resurrection. Many today, for whatever reason, still do not read

His words. The majority back then and many now encounter His spoken words in a Catholic Church filled with Christians worshipping our resurrected Lord Jesus Christ and believing they are receiving Him sacramentally, His body, blood, soul, and divinity in the Eucharist. I am one of them.

One notable exception concerns His disciples and the crowd who first heard the Sermon on the Mount, not in a Church or synagogue but on the mountain that day. As you contemplate the nine Beatitude/Lord's Prayer pairs and the seventy-two questions asked in this primer, I hope you will imagine nine conversations between Jesus and His disciples over three years as they traveled the hills and mountains around Galilee. Imagine the first evening after Jesus gave the famous Sermon and one of the disciples asked the question that surely was on everyone's mind. "Lord, how is it that those persecuted for the sake of righteousness are blessed?" Imagine Jesus answering. "Why have you jumped to the last? First, consider the *'poor in spirit'* and those who pray *'Our Father'* before jumping to the glorious end. First, consider the first man, Adam, and his wife, Eve. First, consider that I will be with you always to the end of the age. Now, get some sleep; we have a mountain to climb tomorrow. While sleeping, dream big dreams, imagine fantastic images, and feel beautiful feelings. The Holy Spirit will bring these dreams, images, and feelings back to your contemplative spirits again and again in the days and years to come for the Spirit, and I want to reveal Your Father, Our Father, My Father who is in heaven."

Of course, others will see different and better ways to unpack the unity inherent in this masterful sermon. Likewise, others will recall other verses from Matthew's gospel, the other gospels, and the rest of the New and Old Testament, which point to, typify, exemplify, and clarify the Beatitudes and the Our Father. I hope you will discover more, and I would love to hear this, for I believe that all of God's revelations, handed down in sacred scripture or tradition, can be explored most efficiently by starting with the Sermon that the Word made flesh offered at the start of His earthly ministry.

First Beatitude

*"Blessed are the poor in Spirit, for theirs is
the kingdom of heaven." (Mat. 5:3)*

1. How does the first Beatitude anticipate and prompt the first part of the Lord's Prayer?

3. How does Jesus' teaching on salt and light and letting God receive the glory for my good deeds clarify the first Beatitude? (See Mat. 5:13-16)

5. How does Jesus' teaching on seeking first the kingdom of God and his righteousness guide me to live and pray for the first Beatitude/Prayer pair to manifest in my life? (See Mat. 6:33-34)

7. When might Adam and Eve have heard *"Blessed are the poor in spirit, for theirs is the kingdom of heaven,"* received clarification from God that echoes Matthew 5:13-16 and responded by praying *"Our Father in heaven?"*

First Part of the Prayer

"Our Father who art in heaven." (Mat. 6:9a)

2. How does the first part of the Lord's Prayer clarify the first Beatitude?

4. How does Jesus' teaching on looking for recompense for righteous deeds from God instead of men guide the Church when praying the first part of the Lord's Prayer? (See Mat. 6:1)

6. How does Jesus' birth in Bethlehem in the Judean Mountains guide the Church's understanding of the first Beatitude/Prayer pair? (See Mat. 2:1-2)

8. How does the Sacrament of Baptism empower the Church to live the first Beatitude/Prayer pair?

Suggested Reading: CCC Articles (1213-1284)

Second Beatitude

*"Blessed are they who mourn, for they
will be comforted." (Mat. 5:4)*

1. How does the second Beatitude anticipate and prompt the second part of the Lord's Prayer?

3. How does Jesus' teaching on not abolishing even one letter but fulfilling the law and prophets clarify the second Beatitude? (See Mat. 5:17-20)

5. How does Jesus' teaching on not judging others or being hypocritical guide me to live and pray for the second Beatitude/Prayer pair to manifest in my life? (See Mat. 7:1-5)

7. When might Abel have heard *"Blessed are they who mourn for they will be comforted,"* received clarification from God that echoes Matthew 5:17-20 and responded by praying *"Hallowed be they name?"*

Second Part of the Prayer

"Hallowed be thy name." (Mat. 6:9b)

2. How does the second part of the Lord's Prayer clarify the second Beatitude?

4. How does Jesus' teaching on almsgiving guide the Church when praying the second part of the Lord's Prayer? (See Mat. 6:2-4)

6. How does Jesus' response to Satan's temptation from the top of a very high mountain guide the Church's understanding of the second Beatitude/Prayer pair? (See Mat. 4:8-11)

8. How does the Sacrament of Reconciliation empower the Church to live the second Beatitude/Prayer pair?

Suggested Reading: CCC Articles (1422–1498)

Third Beatitude

"Blessed are the meek, for they will inherit the land." (Mat. 5:5)

1. How does the third Beatitude anticipate and prompt the third part of the Lord's Prayer?

3. How does Jesus' teaching on murder, anger, bringing gifts to the altar, and quickly settling debts clarify the third Beatitude? (See Mat. 5:21-26)

5. How does Jesus' teaching on not giving holy things to dogs and pearls to swine guide me to live and pray for the third Beatitude/Prayer pair to manifest in my life? (See Mat. 7:6)

7. When might Noah have heard *"Blessed are the meek, for they will inherit the earth,"* received clarification from God that sounds like an echo of Matthew 5:21-26 and responded by praying *"Thy kingdom come, thy will be done on earth as it is in heaven?"*

Third Part of the Prayer

"Your kingdom come, your will be done, on earth as in heaven." (Mat. 6:10)

2. How does the third part of the Lord's Prayer clarify the third Beatitude?

4. How does Jesus' teaching on not praying to be seen by men as the hypocrites do or babbling like pagans guide the Church when praying the third part of the Lord's Prayer? (See Mat. 6:5-8)

6. How does Jesus' preaching on a mountain near the Sea of Galilee guide the Church's understanding of the third Beatitude/Prayer pair? (See Mat. 5:2)

8. How does the Sacrament of Confirmation empower the Church to live the third Beatitude/Prayer pair?

Suggested Reading: CCC Articles (1285–1321)

Fourth Beatitude

"Blessed are they who hunger and thirst for righteousness, for they will be satisfied." (Mat. 5:6)

1. How does the fourth Beatitude anticipate and prompt the fourth part of the Lord's Prayer?

3. How does Jesus' teaching on tearing out lusting eyes and cutting off adulterous hands clarify the fourth Beatitude? (See Mat. 5:27-32)

5. How does Jesus' teaching on asking, seeking, knocking, and receiving from God bread and fish instead of stones and snakes guide me to live and pray for the fourth Beatitude/Prayer pair to manifest in my life? (See Mat. 7:7-11)

7. When might Abraham have heard *"Blessed are they who hunger and thirst for righteousness, for they will be satisfied,"* received clarification from God that sounds like an echo of Matthew 5:21-26 and responded by praying, *"Give us this day our daily bread? "*

Fourth Part of the Prayer

"Give us today our daily bread" (Mat. 6:11)

2. How does the fourth part of the Lord's Prayer clarify the fourth Beatitude?

4. How does Jesus' teaching on fasting guide the Church when praying the fourth part of the Lord's Prayer? (See Mat. 6:16-18)

6. How does Jesus' going to pray on a mountain by Himself after learning of John the Baptist's death and His miraculous feeding of five thousand guide the Church's understanding of the fourth Beatitude/Prayer pair? (See Mat. 14:13-23)

8. How does the Sacrament of Holy Communion empower the Church to live the fourth Beatitude/Prayer pair?

Suggested Reading CCC Articles (1322 – 1419)

Fifth Beatitude

"Blessed are the merciful, for they will be shown mercy." (Mat. 5:7)

1. How does the fifth Beatitude anticipate and prompt the fifth part of the Lord's Prayer?

3. How does Jesus' teaching on not swearing by heaven, earth, Jerusalem, or my head clarify the fifth Beatitude? (See Mat. 5:33-37)

5. How does Jesus' teaching on doing to others what I would have them do to me guide me to live and pray for the fifth Beatitude/Prayer pair to manifest in my life? (See Mat. 7:12)

7. When might Jacob/Israel and his twelve sons have heard *"Blessed are the merciful, for they will be shown mercy,"* received clarification from God that sounds like an echo of Matthew 5:33-37 and responded by praying *"Forgive us our trespasses as we forgive those who trespass against us?"*

Fifth Part of the Prayer

"And forgive us our debts, as we forgive our debtors" (Mat. 6:12)

2. How does the fifth part of the Lord's Prayer clarify the fifth Beatitude?

4. How does Jesus' repetition of this part of the prayer and linking it to *'your heavenly Father'* guide the church when praying the fifth part of the Lord's Prayer? (See Mat. 6:14-15)

6. How does Jesus' healing of the lame, blind, deformed, mute, and many others on a mountain near Galilee guide the Church's understanding of the fifth Beatitude/Prayer pair? (See Mat. 15:29-32)

8. How does the Sacrament of Holy Matrimony empower the Church to live the fifth Beatitude/Prayer pair?

Suggested Reading: CCC Articles (1601 – 1666)

Sixth Beatitude

"Blessed are the clean of heart, for they will see God." (Mat. 5:8)

1. How does the sixth Beatitude anticipate and prompt the sixth part of the Lord's Prayer?

3. How does Jesus' teaching on going two when asked to go one mile, giving a tunic and cloak when sued for a cloak, turning the other cheek, and not resisting evil clarify the sixth Beatitude? (See Mat. 5:38-42)

5. How does Jesus' teaching on entering through the narrow gate guide me to live and pray for the sixth Beatitude/Prayer pair to manifest in my life? (See Mat. 7:13-14)

7. When might Moses and Israel have heard *"Blessed are the clean of heart, for they shall see God,"* received clarification from God that sounds like an echo of Matthew 5:38-42 and responded by praying *"And do not subject us to the final test?"*

Sixth Part of the Prayer

"And do not subject us to the final test" (Mat. 6:13a)

2. How does the sixth part of the Lord's Prayer clarify the sixth Beatitude?

4. How does Jesus' teaching on storing treasures in heaven, light, darkness, and the eye being the lamp of the body guide the Church when praying the sixth part of the Lord's Prayer? (See Mat. 6:19-23)

6. How does Jesus' transfiguration in front of Peter, James, and John on a high mountain guide the Church's understanding of the sixth Beatitude/Prayer pair? (See Mat. 17:1-9)

8. How does the Sacrament of Anointing of the Sick empower the Church to live the sixth Beatitude/Prayer pair?

Suggested Reading: CCC Articles (1499 – 1532)

Seventh Beatitude

"Blessed are the peacemakers, for they will be called children of God." (Mat. 5:9)

1. How does the seventh Beatitude anticipate and prompt the seventh part of the Lord's Prayer?

3. How does Jesus' teaching on being a child of God by loving my enemies and praying for those who persecute me clarify the seventh Beatitude? (See Mat. 5:43-45)

5. How does Jesus' teaching on discerning good and false prophets by the good and bad fruit they bear guide me to live and pray for the seventh Beatitude/Prayer pair to manifest in my life? (See Mat. 7:15-20)

7. When might David and Israel have heard *"Blessed are the peacemakers, for they will be called children of God,"* received clarification from God that sounds like an echo of Matthew 5:43-47 and responded by praying *"But deliver us from evil?"*

Seventh Part of the Prayer

"But deliver us from the evil one." (Mat. 6:13b)

2. How does the seventh part of the Lord's Prayer clarify the seventh Beatitude?

4. How does Jesus' teaching on being unable to serve God and mammon guide the Church when praying the seventh part of the Lord's Prayer? (See Mat. 6:24)

6. How does Jesus' teaching on the Mount of Olives before and after His triumphal entry into Jerusalem guide the Church's understanding of the seventh Beatitude/Prayer pair? (See Mat. 21:1, Mat. 24:3-16)

8. How does the Sacrament of Holy Orders empower the Church to live the seventh Beatitude/Prayer pair?

Suggested Reading: CCC Articles (1533-1560)

The Order of the Mass

Introductory Rites	Entrance Greeting Penitential Act Glory to God Collect	
The Liturgy of the Word	First Reading Responsorial Psalm Second Reading (on Sundays and solemnities) Gospel Acclamation Gospel Homily Profession of Faith (on Sundays, solemnities, and special occasions) Universal Prayer	In the readings and prayers of the liturgy of the word, Jesus speaks to His listening Church which responds with faith at the appointed times. The Beatitudes, as Jesus' first words in the Sermon on the Mount, contain everything Jesus would go on to teach about how to possess the kingdom of heaven.
The Liturgy of the Eucharist	Presentation of the Gifts and Preparation of the Altar Prayer over the Offerings	In the readings and actions of the priest, acting in the person of Christ, and the Church responding as His bride, the daily Mass actuates in every place and time the Sacrifice of Calvary and gives the Church a foretaste of the Wedding Supper of the Lamb. As Christ, the Head, and the Church,

	Eucharistic Prayer • Preface • Holy, Holy, Holy • First half of the prayer, including the Consecration • Second half of the prayer ends with a doxology (not the one after the Lord's prayer) ***The Lord's Prayer with the doxology following the Lord's prayer*** Sign of Peace Lamb of God Communion Prayer after Communion	the Body, move towards intimate Eucharistic union, they pray for the manifestation of the Beatitudes on earth as they move towards heaven. The *embolism*, said by the priest in the person of Christ, joins Jesus' prayer with the Church's prayer at a critical juncture in the Beatitudes' manifestation, right before the Church will willingly suffer for righteousness. Only in unity with the body, soul, humanity, and divinity of Christ can she accomplish God's will in this suffering.
Concluding Rites	Optional announcements Greeting and Blessing Dismissal	

https://www.usccb.org/prayer-and-worship/the-mass/order-of-mass

Eighth Beatitude

"Blessed are they who are persecuted for the sake of righteousness, for theirs is the kingdom of heaven." (Mat. 5:10)

1. How does the eighth Beatitude anticipate and prompt the embolism?

3. How does Jesus' teaching to not love like tax collectors and pagans clarify the embolism? (See Mat. 5:46-47)

5. How does Jesus' teaching on doing the will of His Father in heaven guide me to live and pray for the eighth Beatitude/embolism pair to manifest in my life? (See Mat. 7:21-23)

7. When might John the Baptist/the Church's clergy have heard *"Blessed are they who are persecuted for the sake of righteousness, for theirs is the kingdom of heaven,"* and learned to respond by praying the embolism?

Embolism

"Deliver us, Lord, we pray, from every evil, graciously grant peace in our days, that, by the help of your mercy, we may be always free from sin and safe from all distress, as we await the blessed hope and the coming of our Savior, Jesus Christ."

2. How does the embolism clarify the eighth Beatitude?

4. How does Jesus' teaching on being totally dependent on God for all its needs guide the Church when praying the embolism? (See Mat. 6:25-30)

6. How does Jesus 'crucifixion on Golgotha, Mount Calvary, guide the Church's understanding of the eighth Beatitude/embolism pair? (See Mat. 27:33)

8. How do all seven Sacraments empower the Church to live the eighth Beatitude/embolism pair?

Suggested Reading: CCC Articles (1076 – 1199)

Ninth Beatitude

"Blessed are you when they insult you and persecute you and utter every kind of evil against you [falsely] because of me." (Mat. 5:11)

1. How does Jesus's ninth Beatitude anticipate and prompt the doxology?

3. How does Jesus' teaching to *"Be perfect, just as your heavenly Father is perfect"* clarify the ninth Beatitude? (See Mat. 5:48)

5. How does Jesus' teaching on acting on his words in the Sermon on the Mount guide me to live and pray for the ninth Beatitude/Prayer pair to manifest in my life? (See Mat. 7:24-27)

7. How does the Mass recapitulate and control salvation history?

Doxology

*"For thine is the kingdom, and the power, and
the glory, now and forever, Amen!"*

2. How does the doxology clarify the ninth Beatitude?

4. How does Jesus' teaching on not worrying as the pagans do about having something to eat, drink or wear encourage the Church when praising God in the doxology? (See Mat. 6:31-32)

6. How does Jesus' teaching on a mountain after His resurrection that *"All power in heaven and on earth has been given to me,"* and His command to *"make disciples of all nations baptizing them in the name of the Father, and of the Son, and of the holy Spirit"* guide the Church's understanding of the ninth Beatitude/Prayer pair and its mission? (See Mat. 28:16-20)

8. How do Jesus' words, *"Thus they persecuted the prophets who were before you,"* lead the Church to search for Jesus by contemplating the Old and New Testament Saints as it continues reading Matthew's gospel? (See Mat. 5:12)

Suggestion: Contemplate, write, and act out daily your response to Jesus' call to suffer joyfully for righteousness.

The End of the Sermon on the Mount

*"Everyone who listens to these words of mine and **acts** on them will be like a wise man who built his house on rock. The rain fell, the floods came, and the winds blew and buffeted the house. But it did not collapse; it had been set solidly on rock. And everyone who listens to these words of mine but does **not act** on them will be like a fool who built his house on sand. The rain fell, the floods came, and the winds blew and buffeted the house. And it collapsed and was completely ruined." (Mat. 7:24-27)*

When Jesus describes those who ***act*** and those who do ***not act*** on His words, He indicates that He has already finished His teaching on possessing the kingdom of heaven, the central theme of the Sermon on the Mount. Recall that *the poor in spirit* of the first Beatitude and those who *suffer for the sake of righteousness* of the eighth Beatitude; these are the ones who are *blessed*, *for theirs is the kingdom of heaven*. The description of those who act and those who do not act on His words does not reside within the body of that teaching. It describes, rather, the responses of the two groups to what Jesus taught from Matthew 5:3 through Matthew 7:23 and the inevitable and eternal consequences of those responses thereafter. Of course, technically speaking, every word from Matthew 5:3 through 7:27, every word in between, is part of the Sermon on the Mount. Still, by summarizing these *words of mine* and then issuing the admonition to act on them, Jesus has set apart the last three verses of the sermon from *the rest of the sermon*. I suspect some readers wonder why I am focusing on this distinction. Why is it important? We find the answer in a careful meditation of the words which conclude *the rest of the sermon*, the last words He speaks before He issues the admonition, what I believe are the final words in the Sermon on the Mount describing how to possess the kingdom of heaven. Let's look at them now.

"Not everyone who says to me, 'Lord, Lord,' will enter the kingdom of heaven, but only the one who does the will of my Father in heaven. Many will say to me on that day, 'Lord, Lord, did we not prophesy in your name? Did we not drive out demons in your name? Did we not do mighty deeds in your name?' Then I will declare to them solemnly, 'I never knew you. Depart from me, you evildoers." (Matthew 7:21-23)

To understand what Jesus has done with these final words, we must put them in the context of the preceding words that He spoke, that is the rest of the Sermon on the Mount. We don't need to do an exhaustive analysis of the sermon to see my point. We can see it by focusing on Jesus' use of pronouns before referring to God as Father and how Jesus emphasizes certain statements He was about to make throughout the sermon.

Jesus spoke of God as *Father* seventeen times in the Sermon on the Mount- fifteen times saying **your** *Father/heavenly Father,*- one time saying **Our** *Father,* - and one time saying **My** *Father.* Clearly, Jesus taught His followers to think of God as a Father. In his gospel, Mark emphasized how Jesus modeled this intimate way of crying out to God in his portrayal of Jesus' agony in the garden. *"Abba, Father, all things are possible to you. Take this cup away from me, but not what I will but what you will." Abba*, the Aramaic word for *Father,* conveys a relationship of deep personal trust, more childlike than adultlike. This is how we should understand Jesus' use of the phrase *"they will be called children of God"* when referring to the peacemakers in the seventh Beatitude.

Jesus then identifies with His Church by teaching her to pray *Our Father,* calling to mind the intimacy we enjoy in our relationship with God. *Jesus* is calling us brothers. As a Church, we approach God together or very weakly at best. We are Christians in the plural sense as much as we are Christians singularly. And we approach God with Jesus, or very weakly at best, nay, not at all.

Concerning intimacy with God, we must note that when the Priest recites the embolism, speaking *'In Christi,'* he moves the Church's prayer to a deeper level of intimacy. Why? Because- He, Christ/ he, the Priest *in Christi*, calls the Church to understand that He/ Christ is praying this prayer with us at that moment, spiritually and physically, present entirely as one person, body and soul, human and divine. The timing couldn't be more perfect, for the Priest in the epiclesis has just consecrated the bread and wine, and Jesus has just entered our midst in His full humanity and divinity. Not only this, but we have just reached the eighth Beatitude and heard its call to suffer joyfully. What better time to encourage us with His intimate presence among us?

Continuing to look at Jesus' use of *Father* in the sermon, He will refer to God as *your Father* seven more times in the

Sermon on the Mount following the prayer, after which He refers to God as *Father* for the last time, saying, *My Father,* a switch surely intended. It is as if Jesus has suddenly, almost jealously, grabbed hold of His Father, lest any would take for granted the infinite love He offers. We should not call God *Our Father* casually. We should prepare ourselves to call Him *Our Father* in all circumstances, even those calling us to suffer-suffering is the topic of the eighth and ninth Beatitudes, and we have just arrived there in our analysis of the Beatitude/Lord's Prayer pairs.

We now focus on the times in the Sermon on the Mount when Jesus emphasized the importance of something He was about to say, which He did directly by simply announcing He was about to speak something we must hear. Eleven times in the Sermon on the Mount, Jesus said, *"**I say** to you,* or *Amen **I say** to you"* which emphasized the need to listen even more. It is the same as a professor stopping in the middle of presenting his thesis and saying, *"Hey, pay attention to what I am about to say."* Yes, we must revere and obey every word He speaks, especially those He precedes with special emphasis.

Jesus used a second phrase to emphasize something He was about to say, ***I tell** you.* He used this phrase three times- the first time- *"**I tell** you, unless your righteousness surpasses that of the scribes and Pharisees, you will not enter into the kingdom of heaven."* (Matthew 5:20) We see an emphatic rebuttal of those He calls hypocrites. They surely had the habit of *telling* people what they must do to earn their way into heaven. Jesus used their words against them, setting Himself in opposition to them, an opposition that would widen as His ministry continued.

Jesus used the phrase ***I tell** you* two more times, notably near the end of His use of any words of emphasis. We see this in the sermon when He provides comfort; first, in Matthew 6:25- *"**I tell** you, do not worry about your life, what you will eat [or drink], or about your body, what you will wear"*- and again in Matthew 6:29-30- *"**I tell** you that not even Solomon in all his splendor was clothed like one of them. If God so clothes the grass of the field, which grows today and is thrown into the oven tomorrow, will he not much more provide for you, O you of little faith?"* His use of the phrase ***I tell** you* as the thirteenth and fourteen of fifteen times that He would emphasize what He was about to say further escalates the importance of His words. We understand from this that His words are reaching a crescendo.

We now focus on the fifteenth and last time in the Sermon on the Mount that Jesus emphasized what He was about to say. It occurs in the last three verses of the words He spoke before describing the wise and foolish builders. Note, He has just switched jealously from calling God *Your* and *Our Father* to *My Father*. Had we been listening to Him on the mountain that day, I believe we would have seen a certain flare in His eyes, felt the gravity of His presence, and heard a passion in His voice, ***My Father*** - see how He sets us up for what follows. No longer saying *I say to you* or *I tell you,* as important as those emphasizing words are- but now He says it with definitive finality, *"**I will declare** to them solemnly." (Matthew 7:23a)* He has led his listeners/us to the precipice, to the point of no return, to the point when we must decide and has just given us this ominous warning.

*"Not everyone who **says** to me, 'Lord, Lord,' will enter the kingdom of heaven, but only the one who **does** the will of my Father in heaven. Many will say to me on that day, 'Lord, Lord, did we not prophesy in your name? Did we not drive out demons in your name? Did we not do mighty deeds in your name?'" (Matthew 7:21-22)*

The sobering part of this warning is that those to whom He speaks think they know Him. They call Him *Lord,* not once but twice. More chilling still- they can give a litany of what they have done. They acted. They were doers, not mere listeners. However, their actions, as meritorious as they conceived them to be, were Pharisaical, done as self-righteous hypocrites for men to see in public, not for God to see in the private place of their heart. And thus, sadly, do they hear Him say, *"I never knew you. Depart from me, you evildoers." (Matthew 7:23b)* He only refers to them in the second person, calls them '*you*' when telling them to depart from Him, for, while they knew of Him, they did not know Him intimately, and He then defines who they are, calling them '*evildoers.*'

Continuing with Jesus' use of second and third-person pronouns, we see the same theme at the very beginning of the sermon, with the nine *Blessed are* statements. We note the switch in the nine Beatitudes in how He refers to us, His listeners who act in faith. In the first eight Beatitudes, Jesus spoke impersonally to anyone and everyone in the third person, saying *"Blessed are the poor, they who mourn, the meek, they who hunger and thirst for righteousness, the merciful, the clean of heart, the peacemakers, they who suffer for the sake of righteousness."* But in the ninth Beatitude, after the Church, led by Christ to pray the embolism, after this prayer, Jesus switched to the personal second person, saying,

*"Blessed are **you** when they insult **you** and persecute **you** and utter every sort of evil against **you**, falsely, because of me. Rejoice and be glad, for **your** reward will be great in heaven. Thus they persecuted the prophets who were before **you**." (Matthew 5:11-12, emphasis mine)*

Six times, Jesus emphasizes His personal relationship with those who travel this intimate journey of suffering with Him. And if we imagine and feel the passion in Christ, the bridegroom's words of comfort, so too must we imagine and feel the passion in the response of His Bride. See how she responds.

*For **thine** is the kingdom, and the power, and the glory, now and forever, Amen!!!*

Sermon on the Mount Cross-verse Puzzle

Beatitude	Prayer	Beatitude Clarified	Prayer Clarified	Beatitude/ Prayer Clarified
5:3	6:9a	5:13-16	6:1	6:33-34
5:4	6:9b	5:17-20	6:2-4	7:1-5
5:5	6:10	5:21-26	6:5-8	7:6
5:6	6:11	5:27-32	6:16-18	7:7-11
5:7	6:12	5:33-37	6:14-15	7:12
5:8	6:13a	5:38-42	6:19-23	7:13-14
5:9	6:13b	5:43-45	6:24	7:15-20
5:10	embolism	5:46-47	6:25-30	7:21-23
5:11-12a	doxology	5:48	6:31-32	7:24-27

5:12b calls us to contemplate the prophets before us

References

Except for the Lord's Prayer, which is given in the words said in Mass used by the United States Conference of Catholic Bishops (USCCB), all scripture quotations have been taken from New American Bible Revised Edition ("NABRE"). https://bible.usccb.org/bible

Catechism of the Catholic Church 2nd ed., 1997 https://www.usccb.org/sites/default/files/flipbooks/catechism/II/#zoom=z

www.ingramcontent.com/pod-product-compliance
Lightning Source LLC
Chambersburg PA
CBHW070036040426
42333CB00040B/1698